First Peoples of Asia

Ainu of Japan
Bali Aga of Indonesia
Karen of Burma

TRISHA SERTORI

MACMILLAN LIBRARY

First published in 2009 by
MACMILLAN EDUCATION AUSTRALIA PTY LTD
15–19 Claremont Street, South Yarra 3141

Visit our website at www.macmillan.com.au or go directly to www.macmillanlibrary.com.au

Associated companies and representatives throughout the world.

National Library of Australia Cataloguing-in-Publication entry

Sertori, Trisha.
Of Asia: Ainu of Japan, Bali Aga of Indonesia, Karen of Burma / Trisha Sertori.

ISBN 978 1 4202 6800 3
Sertori, Trisha. First peoples series
Includes index.
For primary school age.
Ainu - Social life and customs - Juvenile literature.
Ainu - Civilization - Juvenile literature.
Bali-Aga (Indonesian people) - Social life and customs - Juvenile literature.
Bali-Aga (Indonesian people) - Civilization - Juvenile literature.
Karen (Southeast Asian People) - Social life and customs - Juvenile literature.
Karen (Southeast Asian People) - Civilization - Juvenile literature.

952.004946

Edited by Anna Fern
Text design by Stella Vassiliou and Cristina Neri, Canary Graphic Design
Cover design by Stella Vassiliou and Cristina Neri, Canary Graphic Design
Page layout by Cristina Neri, Canary Graphic Design
Photo research by Legend Images
Maps by Damien Demaj, DEMAP

Printed in China

Acknowledgements
Front cover photographs: Group of Balinese women and young girls in traditional costumes during the tradition mekare-kare that is fight the screw pine, photo © Jean-Christophe Godet/Alamy/Photolibrary, **top left**; Japan Hokkaido Ainu man, photo © Tibor Bognar/Alamy/Photolibrary, **top right**; Karen family having dinner Chiang Mai Thailand, photo © Images & Stories/Alamy/Photolibrary, **bottom**.

Background image courtesy of Istockphoto/enviromantic.

Photos courtesy of:
Auscape International/ Karen Gowlett-Holmes, **19**; AFP/Getty Images, **18**; STR/AFP/ Getty Images, **13**; Khin Maung Win/ AFP/Getty Images, **26**, **29**; Hulton Archives/Getty Images, **10**, **11**; Marie Mathelin/Roger Viollet/Getty Images, **15**; Jerry Alexander/Stone/Getty Images, **23**; National Geographic Stock/Natalie B. Fobes, **12**; National Geographic Stock/Gina Martin, **25**; © Amana Images Inc./Alamy/Photolibrary, **6**; © Tibor Bognar/Alamy/Photolibrary, **7**, **8**; © dbimages/Alamy/ Photolibrary, **20**, **21**; © Jean-Christophe Godet/Alamy/Photolibrary, **16**; © Mike Goldwater/Alamy/Photolibrary, **28**; © Blaine Harrington III/Alamy/Photolibrary, **17**; © Images & Stories/Alamy/Photolibrary, **24**; © Frantisek Staud/Alamy/ Photolibrary, **9**; © V1/Alamy/Photolibrary, **27**; © Chris Willson/Alamy/Photolibrary, **30**; Shutterstock, **4**, **14**, **22**.

While every care has been taken to trace and acknowledge copyright, the publisher tenders their apologies for any accidental infringement where copyright has proved untraceable. Where the attempt has been unsuccessful, the publisher welcomes information that would redress the situation.

Internet addresses
At the time of printing, the Internet addresses appearing in this book were correct. Owing to the dynamic nature of the Internet, however, we cannot guarantee that all these addresses will remain correct.

Contents

Glossary words

When a word is printed in **bold**, you can look up its meaning in the Glossary on page 31.

First peoples of the world

First peoples are the original inhabitants of a region. They have developed their own **culture**, traditions, laws and way of life over thousands of years. First peoples are also called **indigenous people**.

Today, there are more than 370 million indigenous people living all around the world, from the icy Arctic Circle to the deserts of Australia. Many indigenous cultures, however, have been damaged or destroyed by **colonists** who have moved onto indigenous peoples' lands.

This book will introduce you to some first peoples of the world. You will discover their history, how they live, and how they have survived in a changing world.

This Karen woman is indigenous to Burma.

"The United Nations says"

"*Indigenous peoples have suffered from historic injustices as a result of the **colonisation** and **dispossession** of their lands, territories and **resources**. The **United Nations** Declaration on the Rights of Indigenous Peoples recognises the urgent need to respect and promote the rights of indigenous peoples and their lands, territories and resources.*"

Adapted from the United Nations Declaration on the Rights of Indigenous Peoples, 2007

First peoples of Asia

There are hundreds of first peoples across Asia. In this book, we will meet:

- the Ainu people, from Japan
- the Bali Aga people, from the island of Bali, in Indonesia
- the Karen people, from Burma (Myanmar).

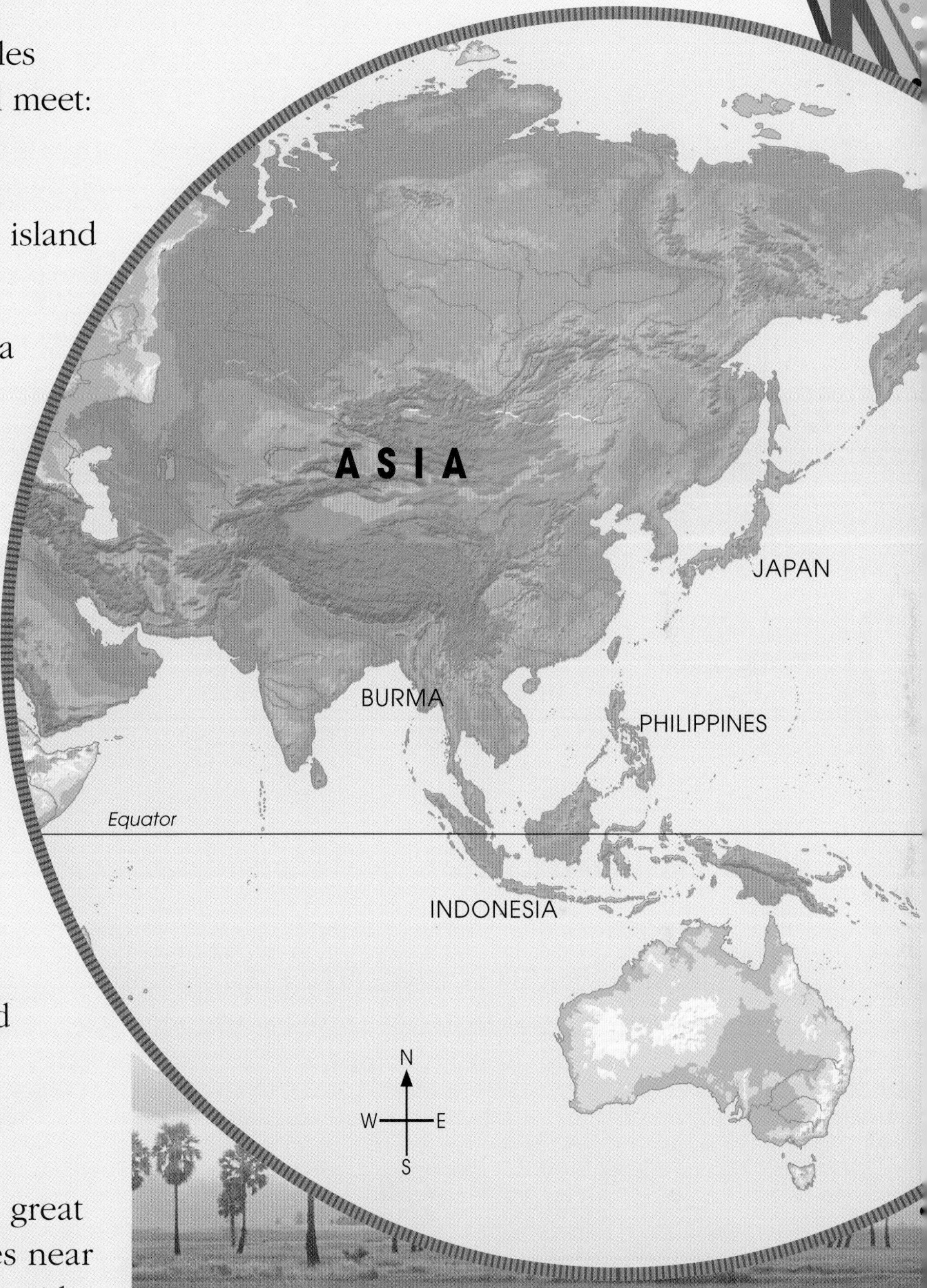

The region

Asia stretches from the Red Sea in the west, to the Philippines in the far east, and includes Asian Russia, China, India and Southeast Asia.

The Ainu people live in Japan, in far eastern Asia. The Bali Aga and Karen peoples live in Southeast Asia. Southeast Asia is made up of **archipelagoes**, such as Indonesia, and mainland countries, such as Thailand.

Climates

The climate across Asia varies a great deal. Much of Southeast Asia lies near the Equator. Here it is **tropical**, with just two seasons, the wet and the dry. Northern regions of Asia, including Japan, are **temperate**, with four seasons – winter, spring, summer and autumn.

Ainu of Japan

For thousands of years, the Ainu people lived on Sakhalin Island, Hokkaido and the Kurile Islands. Most Ainu today live in Hokkaido.

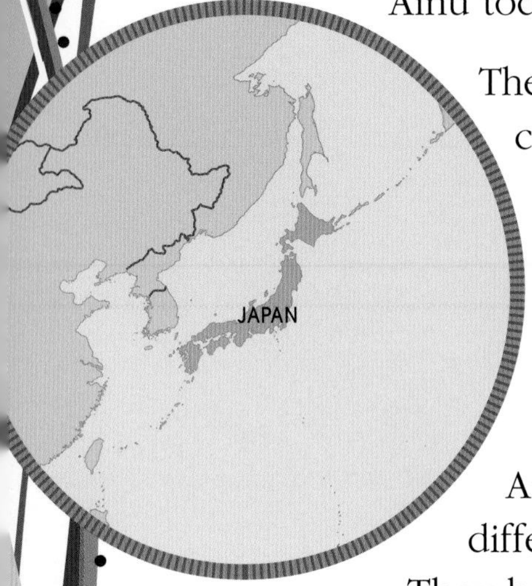

The Japanese have colonised Hokkaido for 400 years. Ainu land was sold to colonists and many of their cultural practices were banned.

Ainu are physically very different to other Japanese. They have curly hair and round eyes. Ainu men grow beards and moustaches.

The region

Hokkaido has snow-covered mountains, many lakes, rocky coastlines and beaches. Towns are covered by snow in winter.

In winter, the average temperature on Hokkaido is minus 12 degrees Celsius. In summer, the temperature is around 22 degrees.

Population

Between 24 000 to 50 000 Ainu live in Hokkaido today. More than 120 million Japanese people also live there.

Language

Today, there are only about 16 Ainu speakers. **Linguists** are now trying to preserve the language.

Did you know?

Ainu parents wanted their children to learn the Ainu language. In 1982, Ainu opened an Ainu language childcare centre. The Japanese Government banned Ainu language in the centre.

Winters in Hokkaido are freezing.

You can find out more about the Ainu at http://en.wikipedia.org/wiki/Ainu_people

Traditional Ainu life

Traditionally, Ainu were hunter-gatherers and farmers.

Food

The Ainu fished for salmon, hunted small animals and collected berries and herbs. They farmed wheat, barley, millet, rice, melons and safflower.

Housing

Early Ainu houses, called *chise*, were built over a pit. The houses had wooden posts and grass walls. Inside was a long room with a fireplace in the centre. Floors were covered with grass mats.

Clothing

Most Ainu clothing is similar in shape to kimonos. Traditional Ainu clothing is made from a fibre from the inner skin of Japanese elm tree bark, called *bast*. Bast is woven to make coats called *attus*, often decorated with **geometric** embroidery in blues and whites. Salmon skin and animal furs were also used for clothing. Salmon skin was prized because it was lightweight and waterproof.

Did you know?
Special embroidered patterns on Ainu clothing are believed to keep evil spirits away.

A young Ainu man wears traditional clothing decorated with geometric designs.

Ainu society

Ainu villages, called *kotan*, were made up of between three and twenty houses. Kotans were usually near rivers or streams close to the sea. Homes were the centre of Ainu life.

Ainu families

Some Ainu families shared their home with grandparents and great grandparents. At first, a young wife would move into her husband's family home. They would then build a new home to start their family.

Family **ancestry** was traced through symbols. Men had animal symbols, such as a bear. Women had tattoos on their forearms. These symbolised different families.

Government

Ainu today are governed by the Japanese Government. In the past, each village had three chiefs. Chief titles were passed from father to son. Chiefs made decisions for village welfare.

Crimes were judged by all village members. Beatings were often given as punishment. Punishment for murder was amputation of ears and nose.

Did you know?

Dogs were kept as pets by the Ainu. Dogs protected families and helped in hunting.

Traditional Ainu houses have grass walls and thatched roofs.

Ainu learning for life

Traditionally, Ainu children were taught by their parents and community.

Learning traditional skills

There was much for young Ainu children to learn. They learned to:

- farm
- hunt, fish and gather forest foods
- weave and embroider
- prepare skins for clothing
- cook.

Learning about religion

The Ainu people believed nature was full of gods and goddesses who needed to be recognised in prayer. Children learnt about the gods from their grandparents during storytelling.

Modern education

Since the 1900s, Ainu children have been going to Japanese schools. Lessons are in the Japanese language, so Ainu children rarely hear their traditional language. In the recent past, many Ainu children pretended to be Japanese. This was because they suffered **discrimination** at school.

Did you know?

In one traditional game, Ainu children tied clam shells to their feet. When they ran, the shells made a clop-clop noise like horses' hooves.

The United Nations says

"Indigenous peoples and individuals are free and equal to all other peoples and individuals and have the right to be free from any kind of discrimination, in the exercise of their rights, in particular that based on their indigenous origin or identity."

Article 2 of the United Nations Declaration on the Rights of Indigenous Peoples, 2007

These Ainu girls go to Japanese schools and dress in modern clothing.

Ainu celebrations and rituals

The Ainu people believe that everything has a spirit that helps people. Spirits are in animals, plants, cooking pots, household utensils, clothing and tools. These spirits are all celebrated.

Spirit sending

An important Ainu celebration was called the spirit-sending festival. A baby bear was caught and Ainu prayed, danced and sang to the cub for three days. The bear was then killed to release his spirit. The bear **ritual** is now banned.

Tattoos

Tattooing was an Ainu ritual to mark different stages in life. When young girls were old enough to marry, they had their lips tattooed. The government banned lip tattooing, however some Ainu still tattoo their lips.

Funeral rites

Ainu believed the dead return to the spirit world. Ainu were buried with tools they used in life so they could use them in the spirit world. Mourners prayed that the deceased would have an easy journey to the spirit world.

Traditionally, young Ainu women who were ready to marry had their lips tattooed.

Ainu women, with their tattooed lips and traditional clothing, weave a floor mat.

Ainu arts and crafts

The best known Ainu craft is the richly embroidered elm bark attus coat.

Abstract patterns

The Ainu banned making pictures or sculptures of living things, such as birds or trees, or geographical features, such as mountains or rivers. They believed everything had a spirit within. To make a picture of a spirit was a sin. Instead, they created beautiful abstract designs to decorate items such as clothing, pottery, knife handles and weapons.

Basketry

Ainu baskets are very similar to the intricate baskets of the Inuit. Some **anthropologists** suggest the Ainu and Inuit may have been related or traded in the past.

Poems and stories

Ancient Ainu stories tell of the gods and the creation of the world. These stories and long poems are called *yukar*.

Did you know?

Kayano Shigeru was an Ainu leader who collected many traditional Ainu crafts, such as poison arrows, canoes and knives during the 1960s. He believed if these items were not preserved they would be lost to future generations.

Changes to Ainu life

During the past 400 years, Japanese colonists have moved north to Hokkaido, home of the Ainu. The Ainu were also moved from their other traditional lands on Sakhalin Island to Hokkaido following World War II.

The Japanese colonists believed the Ainu should give up their traditions, religion and language and be **assimilated** into the larger Japanese society.

In the past, the Ainu could not openly take part in religious ceremonies, such as this salmon ceremony.

Language lost

Due to their assimilation into Japanese culture, much of the Ainu language has been lost. When languages are lost, much of a culture dies, because histories can no longer be fully told.

Discrimination

Today, the Ainu still suffer discrimination. They are generally less well off than other Japanese and often have less access to education. The Japanese Government has introduced some measures to help the Ainu improve their lives.

"The United Nations says"

"Indigenous peoples and individuals have the right to belong to an indigenous community or nation, in accordance with the traditions and customs of the community or nation concerned. No discrimination of any kind may arise from the exercise of such a right."

Article 9 of the United Nations Declaration on the Rights of Indigenous Peoples, 2007

Ainu men bow on 6 June 2008, when the Japanese Government recognised them as an indigenous people.

Ainu survival

In 1997, the Japanese Government recognised Ainu as indigenous to Hokkaido. Ainu people again began learning their language and culture, following the 1997 Japanese Law for the Promotion of the Ainu Culture and Dissemination and Advocacy for the Traditions of the Ainu, and the Ainu Culture law.

Drowning a village

One of the largest traditional Ainu villages, Nibutani, was flooded to build a reservoir on the Hokkaido coast during 1997. Many Ainu lost their traditional homes and many Ainu **artefacts** were lost. Court cases proved the government had acted illegally by destroying the Ainu village.

Agreement reached

Today, the Ainu have become more politically active, with several **lobby groups** seeking greater recognition and help for the Ainu. Government help could ensure the preservation of the Ainu language and Ainu culture into the future.

Bali Aga of Indonesia

The Bali Aga are among of the earliest inhabitants of the Indonesian island of Bali. They are thought to have lived on the island since around 300 CE.

The region

There are around 100 Bali Aga villages in northeast Bali. The largest and best known are Tenganan and Trunyan. Tenganan is on Bali's eastern slopes near the coast. Trunyan lies on the volcanic slopes of Mount Batur above the volcano's crater lake. Trunyan can only be reached by boat.

Bali is in the Ring of Fire earthquake zone and has regular earthquakes and volcanic eruptions.

Bali lies close to the Equator and has a tropical climate. On the coast, the temperature averages 30 degrees Celsius. In mountain villages, the temperature averages 25 to 28 degrees Celsius.

Language and population

There are around 5000 Bali Aga people. They speak Balinese and Bahasa Indonesia.

Did you know?

The name Bali Aga comes from the **Sanskrit** word for mountain.

Bali Aga villagers live above this lake, on the volcanic slopes of Mount Batur.

Stone is an important building material in the Bali Aga village of Tenganan.

Traditional Bali Aga life

Bali was colonised by Hindus from the island of Java between the 1400s and 1500s. Bali Aga retreated to the mountains to escape the colonists. Bali Aga still live as they did 500 years ago. They use their isolation to protect their culture.

Villages

Bali Aga villages are encircled by stone walls. The cobble-stoned streets follow the contours of the hills. A long house in the centre of the village is used during celebrations.

Houses are built from stone or mud brick. The walls join one house to the next, much like terrace houses. Bali Aga houses are built to withstand earthquakes.

Food

Pigs and goats are raised for meat. Foods such as rice, sweet potatoes, taro, spinach and tropical fruits are farmed.

Clothing

Traditionally, Bali Aga men wear a **sarong**. Women wear a sarong and a lace shirt called a *kebaya*. Young Bali Aga today wear jeans and t-shirts.

Did you know?

Dodal is a delicious Bali Aga sweet made of boiled and thickened jackfruit or banana wrapped in banana leaves.

Bali Aga villagers come together for celebrations.

Bali Aga society

The village is the most important place in the world for the Bali Aga. Villagers all know each other. They work together to grow rice, corn and other crops. They also prepare for celebrations and religious rituals together.

Village heads

The most important people in Bali Aga villages are the Mangku and Bendesa. The Mangku is the religious head who leads prayers and rituals. The Bendesa is the mayor of the village. The Bendesa and the men of the community discuss problems and solutions.

Families

Bali Aga live in extended families of grandparents, parents and children. When women marry, they move to their husband's home. Bali Aga fear having only daughters because when they marry there is no one to care for elderly family members.

Religion

The Bali Aga are Hindus. Hinduism was brought to Indonesia from India around 500 CE. The Bali Aga form of Hinduism is not found anywhere else.

Bali Aga learning for life

Bali Aga believe children need to learn about their culture, religion and traditions. They also believe children need a modern education that offers them jobs in the future.

Traditional education

Until the middle of the 1900s, Bali Aga children were taught by their parents and grandparents. Some learned to read and write religious texts written in Sanskrit on palm leaf books called *lontar*.

Bali Aga children today still learn their culture and traditions from their parents and community. Children of Mangku still learn Sanskrit and study lontar. These children will become Mangku when they grow up.

Learning traditional skills

Girls learn to spin and weave, make Hindu offerings called banten, and cook. Boys learn to farm, play music called gamelan, and carve wood and stone.

Modern education

All Indonesian children, including the Bali Aga, must go to school. Lessons are taught in Bahasa Indonesia, so Bali Aga children must learn to speak that language.

Bali Aga boys learn to play gamelan.

Bali Aga celebrations and rituals

Religious rituals are an important part of Bali Aga life, and throughout the year there are many religious festivities.

Daily offerings

The Bali Aga make offerings to the gods twice daily. Offerings are made of coconut fronds, flowers, incense, rice, fruit and holy water. Offerings are made to Hindu gods and demons. Bali Aga believe demons will not disturb humans if they receive offerings.

Marriages

Bali Aga weddings are community events. Everyone helps to prepare the food, such as dodal. The bride and groom dress in traditional **ikat** fabric.

Funeral rites

The Bali Aga of Trunyan have special funeral rites not found in other Bali Aga villages. Trunyan dead are placed at the foot of a sacred banyan tree. The dead are wrapped in ikat fabric and covered with a bamboo cage. The cage prevents animals such as wild dogs disturbing the bodies. When the bones of the deceased are clean, they are stored with hundreds of other skeletons.

At this Bali Aga cemetery, bones are stored in the shade of a huge banyan tree.

The Bali Aga use hand-operated looms to weave their famous cloth designs.

Bali Aga arts and crafts

Bali Aga believe making art pleases the gods. There are many arts and crafts, including painting, sculpture, weaving and music.

Woven fabrics

The Bali Aga make a fabric called ikat. Ikat is made from fibres from the kapas tree, also called kapok. The fibre is spun and coloured with dyes made from plant roots, flowers and leaves. It is then woven into cloth.

The Bali Aga of Tenganan weave a special cloth called double ikat. Double ikat has the patterns dyed into both the **weft and warp** of the fabric.

Sculptures

Bali Aga carve wood and stones to make religious sculptures. Some of these look like demons or monsters.

Music

Gamelan orchestras are played across Indonesia. Bali Aga play gamelan made from bamboo, wood, bronze and animal skins.

Did you know?

Bali Aga monster carvings are believed to frighten off evil spirits and protect villages and homes.

Changes to Bali Aga life

The Bali Aga have survived several colonisations over the past 600 years. Their isolation protects their culture from many introduced problems.

Javanese

The earliest colonisation of Bali was from Javanese Hindu royal families in the 1400s. They fled Java to escape the change from Hindu to Islam as the state religion. The Bali Aga fled to the mountains and built walled villages to protect themselves from the colonisers.

The Dutch

Holland colonised Indonesia from the late 1700s. By remaining in their isolated villages, the Bali Aga were able to remain apart from the Dutch. The Dutch left during World War II when Japanese armies took control of much of the country.

Tourism and the modern world

The greatest threat to Bali Aga traditional life is from tourism and the modern world. Tourism has introduced money, pollution and cultural breakdown among youth.

"The United Nations says"

"Indigenous peoples have the right to maintain and strengthen their distinct political, legal, economic, social and cultural institutions, while retaining their right to participate fully, if they so choose, in the political, economic, social and cultural life of the State."

Article 5 of the United Nations Declaration on the Rights of Indigenous Peoples, 2007

Tourists buy souvenirs of Bali Aga culture, but also open up Bali Aga culture to the modern world.

This shop in Tenganan sells traditional carved wooden masks to tourists.

Bali Aga survival

Bali Aga continue their cultural practices, despite tourism and colonisation. By building strong communities, Bali Aga are able to access the modern world on their own terms.

Trunyan

The isolated Bali Aga village of Trunyan can only be reached by boat and is far from Bali's tourist destinations. Distance, combined with a strong community desire for cultural preservation, has protected the Bali Aga in Trunyan.

Non-Bali Aga people are banned from living in Trunyan. This prevents tourists from buying holiday homes in the area and protects Bali Aga farming lands.

Tenganan

The village of Tenganan in east Bali has opened its doors to tourism. Villagers sell basketry, carvings and double ikat to tourists. There are strict rules, however, on what visitors can do while in the village.

The Bali Aga of Tenganan are happy to teach outsiders about their culture. Having visitors allows young Bali Aga to practise their English skills and establish businesses around the outer walls of the village that do not harm their culture.

Karen of Burma

The Karen people of Burma **migrated** south from the Mongolia's Gobi Desert more than 2000 years ago. Karen are believed to be Burma's first settlers.

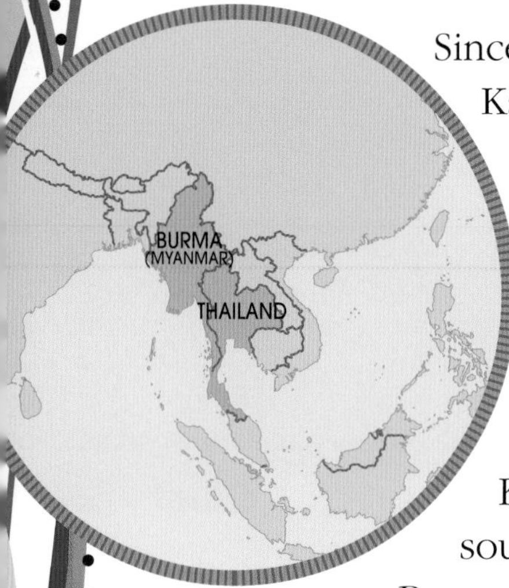

Since settling in Burma, the Karen have been invaded by the Mongolian Mon, the Burmese and the British.

The region

Most Karen live in Karen State in the southeastern hills of Lower Burma and across the border in western Thailand. The Karen call this area *Kawthoolei.*

The climate is tropical, but cooler in the mountains.

Population

Today, more than 10 million Karen live in Burma, where they are the second largest ethnic group. About 400 000 Karen live in Thailand. The Karen make up the largest of the hill tribes in that country.

Language

The Karen people speak three different languages: Sgaw, Pwo and Pa'o. Their languages, however, are not recognised by today's Burmese Government.

Did you know?

Burma was renamed Myanmar in 1989. Many Burmese ethnic groups prefer the name Burma.

The Karen live in the mountains in houses made from rainforest materials.

You can find out more about the Karen at http://www.karen.org/

Traditional Karen life

Traditionally, Karen communities work together to grow crops.

Food

Traditionally, Karen farmed rice and grew vegetables. They also hunted for small animals and fish and gathered forest foods. Foods are flavoured with chilli, spices and fish paste. Families and neighbours often eat meals together.

Housing

Karen housing is built with materials from the forest. Bamboo is used for house frames and thatched roofs are made from grasses. Walls are woven from different coloured bamboos.

Clothing

Traditionally, Karen men and women wear a sarong. Unmarried girls often wear white. After marriage, they weave and wear colourful sarongs. Today, many Karen wear t-shirts and modern dress.

One of the best known groups of Karen are the Paduang women, who wear neck rings. Neck rings make the neck appear long, as the rings push down the collarbone. Other Karen women wear large earrings that stretch the earlobes.

Did you know?

Neck rings are worn to protect women from tiger bites and as decoration.

Young Paduang Karen girls wear brass neck rings.

Karen society

Karen society is matrilineal. This means that families follow their mother's and grandmother's line rather than their father's and grandfather's line. Women **inherit** family property from their mothers.

Karen men and women do not touch unless they are married. Girls, however, are very affectionate with each other, and men and boys often hold hands.

Village government

During times of peace, the Karen have a village chief and council who make many decisions for the village. They also make the laws and enforce punishments when people break traditional laws.

Due to ongoing **civil wars** in Burma, many Karen today are **refugees** living in camps along the Thai border.

Did you know?

Many Karen have teeth blackened by betel nut. Betel nut is made from the leaf of the betel tree crushed with areca palm nuts, rolled into a ball and chewed. Red dye in the betel nut colours lips, teeth and tongue.

Extended Karen families often eat meals together.

Karen learning for life

Traditionally, Karen culture was passed down from generation to generation in stories and songs. Civil war has interrupted traditional education. Skills are now taught in some refugee camps, so that after the war Karen will still have their culture.

Traditional education

For centuries, mothers taught their daughters life skills such as cloth and bamboo weaving, jewellery making and cooking. Karen boys learn from their fathers how to grow rice and vegetables and hunt.

The history of the Karen people is taught in songs and stories. Lullabies of Karen culture and history are sung to babies. Older children join adults around the fire in the evenings when the stories of the past are told.

Modern education

The war prevents some Karen children going to school. Teaching in traditional languages is banned, so Karen education has fallen fall behind that of other Burmese people.

Karen school children learn to make traditional crafts.

Did you know?

The Karen people are recognised as the best elephant trainers in the world. Elephants transport people and goods.

Karen celebrations and rituals

Karen celebrations and rituals follow farming seasons. Each month has a special celebration that is tied to the land.

Courtship

May is the month for rice planting and **courtship**. The village community moves from rice field to rice field and young couples get to know each other. Farmers cook feasts for the village to celebrate the rice plantings.

Marriages

February is the favourite month for weddings. This is also the month when pumpkins, cassava, yams and other vegetables are harvested.

Farming ceremonies

July is the mid-growing season for many plants. Karen hold celebrations to give thanks to the gods for a productive season.

Deaths and new beginnings

Funerals are often held in December when the year's growing season ends. Life begins again in January, when houses are built and women begin weaving and colouring cloths to be used in the coming year.

Did you know?

The Karen year begins with Chinese New Year. Farmlands are prepared for the coming year's growing season.

Karen women dance during New Year celebrations

Karen women weave colourful cloth by hand on a loom.

Karen arts and crafts

The making of Karen arts and crafts has been affected by Burma's 40-year civil war. There were fears the more than 150 000 **displaced** Karen may lose their cultural roots. To preserve their culture, Karen in Mae La refugee camp in Thailand are learning Karen arts, crafts, music and traditional stories.

Wrist tying

In the ancient Karen tradition of wrist tying, white thread is tied around the wrist. This is to chase away evil spirits.

Karen cloth

The patterns in Karen weavings tell different stories.

Some patterns include:

- *Keetee*, a striped pattern with pine tree bark dye
- *Theenga*, insects on water pattern
- *WaeSoLa*, bamboo pattern
- *TaLu*, triangular mountains pattern
- *Ger La Pua Mue Pwa* or housekeeper stripes.

Musical instruments

Instrument-making is a traditional Karen skill being taught in refugee camps today. Some instruments are the harp, bamboo clappers and drums.

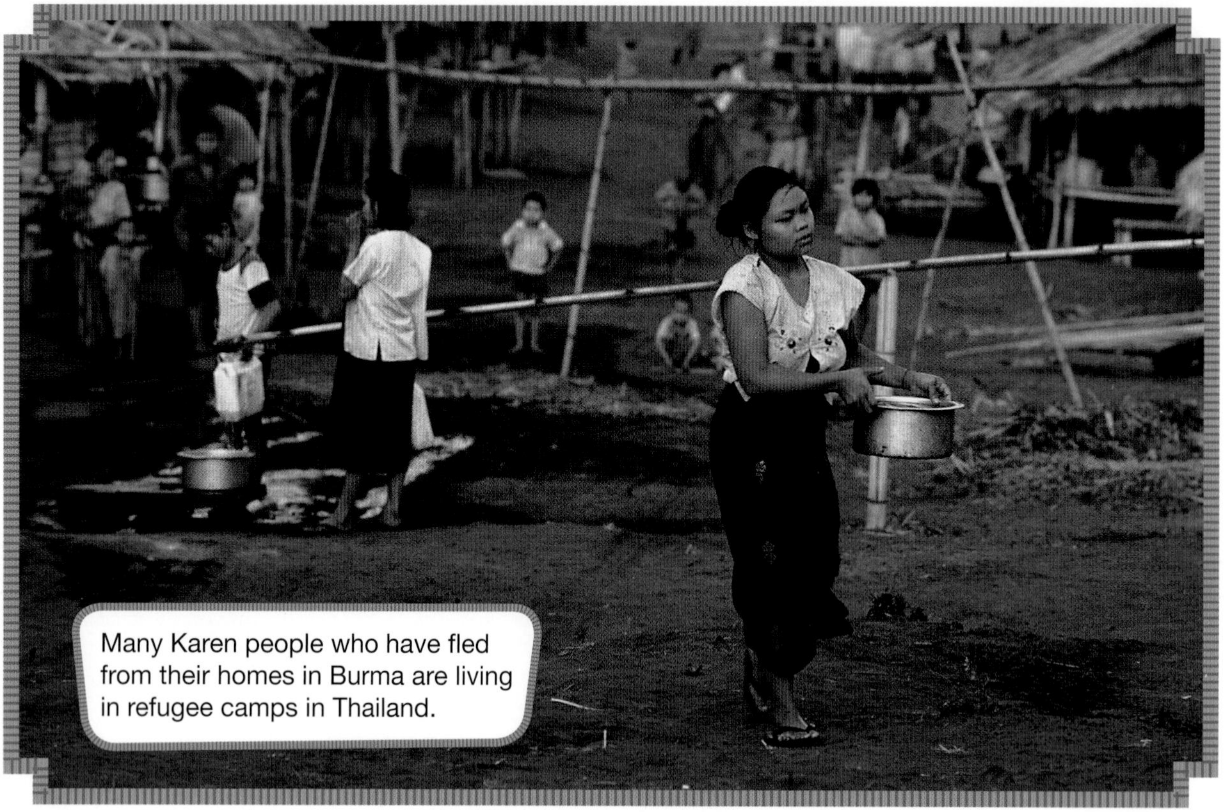

Many Karen people who have fled from their homes in Burma are living in refugee camps in Thailand.

Changes to Karen life

Karen villages traditionally shared work and harvests with all community members. Everyone had enough to eat and was looked after.

Burmese control

Invasions by Mons and Burmese centuries ago changed the Karen way of life, introducing **feudalism**. Karen had few rights, working for the ruling Burmese in return for food. Many fled to the mountains to escape.

The British

The British occupied Burma from 1886 to 1948. Feudalism was reduced and the Karen returned to schools and towns, protected by the British.

Burmese independence

Burma became an **independent nation** in 1948. With independence, Karen hoped their traditional lands would become an independent Karen State. The British, however, recommended the country be one nation made up of Burmese, Karen, Mon and other ethnic groups.

Burma today

The ethnic groups of Burma have been in a state of civil war for the past 40 years. Many ethnic groups, such as the Karen, have fled Burma and are refugees.

Karen survival

After Burma became independent from Britain in 1948, the country became the Union of Burma.

In February 1948, about 400 000 Karen demonstrated, calling for a Karen State. An independent Karen State had been promised by the British during World War II, but was not granted.

Civil war

By 1949, civil war had broken out in Burma because of disagreements between the Burmese and other ethnic groups over territory. The civil war continues. Over the past 50 years, thousands have died or fled to refugee camps along the Thai border.

Military rule

In 1989, a **military coup** overthrew the Burmese Government. Burma was renamed Myanmar. The military still controls the country.

In 2008, hundreds of Burma's Buddhist monks protested Burma's military government. Monks were shot or arrested.

Towards democracy

One of the most famous fighters for **human rights** in Burma is Aung San Suu Kyi. She is the leader of the National League for Democracy party.

People such as Aung San Suu Kyi and leaders of other nations hope Burma will soon become a democratic nation. This would ensure equal rights for all Burmese people.

Under military rule, the people of Burma have no say in who governs their country.

The future for first peoples of Asia

First peoples of Asia face differing issues.

The Ainu of Japan are today recognised as an indigenous people and have the right to maintain their culture. For more than 400 years, however, they faced discrimination and the outlawing of many of their traditional practices. Today, Ainu are rebuilding these traditions.

Indonesia's Bali Aga have been the least damaged by colonialism and the changing world. A policy of isolation has protected their culture, religious practices and traditions. Today, tourism is playing a positive role in that protection. Tourism allows the Bali Aga to be part of a monetary economy on their own terms.

The Karen of Burma still face discrimination, civil war and life in refugee camps. They are working to maintain their culture, despite being a displaced people. Governments around the world are calling for an end to violence in Burma.

First peoples such as the Ainu have had to fight for the right to maintain their culture.

"The United Nations says"

"Indigenous peoples and individuals have the right not to be subjected to forced assimilation or destruction of their culture."

Article 8 of the United Nations Declaration on the Rights of Indigenous Peoples, 2007

Glossary

ancestry earlier generations of family members

anthropologists people who study societies

archipelagoes groups of islands

artefacts items made by humans, such as tools and works of art

assimilated absorbed into a group of people and becoming like them

civil wars wars between different groups within the same country

colonisation taking over land and establishing a settlement, called a colony

colonists people who have moved from their own country to live in a new settlement in another country, called a colony

courtship finding a marriage partner

culture the traditions of a people

discrimination treating a person differently because they belong to a particular category, such as race, religion or gender

displaced forced to leave home

dispossession the taking of land or property from its owners

feudalism a social system where all land was owned by a lord and was farmed by peasants loyal to the lord in return for protection

geometric patterns of regular lines and shapes

human rights rights that all people should have, such as freedom from discrimination because of race, gender or religion

ikat special type of fabric made from threads that have been dyed different colours before weaving

independent nation a nation with its own government, not subject to the authority of another country

indigenous people the first people to live in a region

inherit to receive property or belongings after the death of a family member

linguists people who study languages

lobby groups groups of people who work to promote particular ideas or causes in politics

migrated moved from one place to another

military coup the overthrowing of the government by armed forces

refugees people who have left their home due to persecution, disaster or war

resources the natural products of an area, such as water, food and minerals

ritual special way of doing things, often part of religious ceremonies

Sanskrit ancient language used by Hindus in India

sarong length of fabric worn around the body

temperate mild, without extreme temperatures

tropical hot, humid climate near the Equator

United Nations an international organisation of countries that promotes peace and cooperation

weft and warp the threads strung on a weaving loom

Index